big ideas for
smallgardens

by Emily Young
and
Dave Egbert

Sunset Books
Menlo Park, California

contents

introduction|4

big ideas|8

SUNSET BOOKS

VICE PRESIDENT, GENERAL MANAGER:
Richard A. Smeby

VICE PRESIDENT, EDITORIAL DIRECTOR:
Bob Doyle

DIRECTOR OF OPERATIONS:
Rosann Sutherland

MARKETING MANAGER: Linda Barker

ART DIRECTOR: Vasken Guiragossian

SPECIAL SALES: Brad Moses

STAFF FOR THIS BOOK

SENIOR EDITOR: Ben Marks

ART DIRECTOR: Alice Rogers

PHOTO EDITOR: Eligio Hernandez

COPY EDITOR: Cynthia Rubin

PRODUCTION SPECIALIST: Linda M. Bouchard

PROOFREADER/INDEXER: Jennifer Block Martin

10 9 8 7 6 5 4 3 2 1
First Printing | January 2007
Copyright © 2007, Sunset Publishing Corporation,
Menlo Park, CA 94025

ISBN-13: 978-0-376-03095-5
ISBN-10: 0-376-03095-X
Library of Congress Control Number: 2006932476
Printed in the United States of America

For additional copies of *Big Ideas for Small Gardens* or any other Sunset book, visit us at www.sunsetbooks.com or call 1-800-526-5111.

Cover photograph: Tim Street-Porter
Garden design: Judy Horton; chairs designed by Suzanne Rheinstein and Associates
Cover design: Vasken Guiragossian

Big Ideas for Small Gardens is organized into three main sections. "Big Ideas" takes you on a tour of small gardens—from sunny and shady ones to gardens with room for entertaining or even growing crops. "Big Concepts" focuses on design principles that can be put to use almost anywhere. Finally, "Small Wonders" recommends ground covers, shrubs, vines, and trees that are best suited to small gardens.

Versailles, France

introduction

Some people live on enormous estates where space is unlimited and money is no object. Lucky them. This is a book for the rest of us—folks tucked agreeably into condos and apartments, into duplexes and lofts, into new houses perched on modest lots, and remodeled houses pushed out to the property lines. In suburban neighborhoods across the country, expanses that were once set aside for lush lawns and rambling backyards have become slivers of greensward, while along urban corridors, city dwellers have learned to appreciate the finer points of steel and concrete. We're living in the age of the incredible shrinking garden. Yet couldn't our increasingly fast-paced, oversubscribed lives use a restorative dose of nature? In a word, yes, perhaps now more than ever.

Fortunately, size is a lot like age. It's only a state of mind. Just because you don't own a baronial spread, there's no reason you can't enjoy the intoxicating pleasures and undeniable benefits of a garden: the lovely sights, the wafting scents, the satisfaction of planting something with your own hands and watching it grow. Yes, Virginia (and Ohio and Arizona and Maine), you can transform even the smallest nook or cranny—be it a porch, a patio, a terrace, or a stairway—into a private retreat. So instead of turning green with envy when you visit a great garden, think instead of ways to incorporate the strongest elements of its grand design into your more intimate space back home.

Take Versailles, for example. The French palace of Louis XIV is renowned for its perfectly pruned topiaries and intricately patterned parterres. But let's face facts:

Homegrown parterre

You're not going to replicate it unless you happen to have 2,000 acres, a legion of groundskeepers, and enough royal loot to pay for them. No problem. If this sort of manicured beauty speaks to you, at least you can capture the essence of Versailles by planting boxwood and myrtle and clipping to your heart's content.

Or what about Sissinghurst, the 15th-century English manor whose massive brick walls all but disappear behind a jaw-dropping profusion of blossoms? The white garden alone will make you swoon. OK, chances are that your budget doesn't include a few thousand dollars a month just for flowers.

The good news is, if an abundance of blooming color is your cup of tea, then having a small garden means it won't cost much to plant your own drifts of roses, lilies, delphiniums, or dahlias to spectacular effect.

Villa d'Este, the celebrated Italian landmark, offers a dramatically different model for landscape design with its enchanting array of ancient waterworks that splash, spray, trickle, and cascade. If such watery novelties intrigue you, try some outdoor plumbing of your own: A fountain, a pond, even a rill—a simple channel of water—can bring your garden to cool, refreshing life.

Villa d'Este, Italy

But say you're after a quieter, more contemplative scene. In this case, let Japan's Ryoanji Temple be your inspiration. Just as it artfully evokes rivers and streams with arrangements of rocks and gravel, so too can you set a meditative tone outside your home by raking a bed of sand and decorating it with a few well-placed boulders. Piping in feng shui music is optional.

And nobody says you're limited to the famous gardens of Europe and Japan. Feel free to borrow ideas from American masterpieces such as the shady woodlands of

Backyard waterfall

Winterthur in Delaware, the vegetable beds and fruit orchards of Monticello in Virginia, and the otherworldly cactus-and-succulent tableaux of Lotusland in California. Or let your imagination run wild. It's your fantasy. There's no right and wrong with a garden, only what makes you happy.

Lotusland, California

All you have to do is start thinking that smaller, not bigger, is better, that less really is more, that supersizing can be just as ill-advised for your garden as it is for your diet. Look at it this way: A petite plot means less maintenance, less water, and less expense. Perhaps best of all, spending less time and energy on the care and feeding of your garden means you'll have more time to kick back and savor its rewards. And that's the whole point, isn't it?

Which brings us to a common assumption about small gardens—that because they're small, they're easy to create. Actually, the more compact your area is, the more rigorous you have to be about maximizing the potential of each square inch. Want a few pots of parsley, rosemary, and basil sprouting in a kitchen window? Fine. You can

do that. Prefer a yard with billowing grasses and flowering plants anchored by a piece of sculpture? You can do that, too—if you plan ahead and make the appropriate choices. By concentrating on the quality rather than the quantity of your space, you can turn the tiniest garden into an oasis. The trick is customizing your ideas to fit.

This book is aimed at helping you do exactly that. Intended to inspire and illuminate, it's a portfolio of stylish gardens and a design primer illustrating the amazing range of possibilities that are yours to explore. The goal is to give anyone—do-it-yourselfers, those hiring professionals, and everyone in between—a grounding in the general concepts and some of the latest space-efficient plants and accessories that will allow you to get the most out of your pocket-size space. So if you're ready, let's grow.

Lotusland in a birdbath

big ideas
garden by garden

container gardens ◉ sun gardens ◉ shade gardens ◉ flower gardens ◉ edible gardens
living spaces ◉ rock gardens ◉ water gardens ◉ indoor gardens

Ceramic tiles embellish the risers of these garden steps, but it's the potted plants that introduce living color. Arranged off to one side to keep the way clear, the geraniums and succulents are quickly and easily moved whenever the weather or the traffic pattern changes.

container gardens

Container gardens are versatile role players. They can link interiors and exteriors, accent borders, and soften hard edges. On a balcony or rooftop, where there's no ground to cultivate, they're the star attraction. Around doorways and transition areas, they're the supporting cast, echoing a front court or foreshadowing a yard out back.

Wherever you use containers, fill them with the same plants both indoors and out to help a small garden seem like an extension of the house, and vice versa. You'll also do yourself a favor by pairing containers with complementary plants. Clipped boxwood in a footed bowl offers a classical touch, while dwarf bamboo in a ginger jar strikes an Eastern note.

Pots, urns, and bowls made of terra-cotta, glazed ceramic, stone, metal, and cast concrete make sturdy and long-lasting choices. When weight and space are factors, plastic or fiberglass vessels are smart alternatives. So are baskets for hanging and boxes for window dressing. Whatever your style, avoid mismatched containers in favor of the harmony of those that look alike or share a family resemblance.

Size matters, too. Make sure you leave enough room for healthy roots so that plants won't dry out between watering. And protect them from the worst that nature has to offer by placing them under a deep overhang or near a windbreak.

Containers can hold everything from groundcovers to flowering plants to small trees. When combining several plants in one vessel, a good rule of thumb is to group three types: tall, bushy, and cascading. Such variety represents the world in microcosm, which guarantees a garden in every pot.

Pairing sculptural plants with sleek architectural containers can increase their visual impact. Here, a group of small succulents creates its own miniature landscape.

A trio of understated containers allows these geyserlike grasses to shine rather than compete for attention. Yarrow is a colorful filler between two of the containers. Variations on the cube shape are evident elsewhere in the garden, including the angular forms of a nearby path and pavilion.

Add an element of surprise by recycling old furniture. Here, a profusion of flowers, including Santa Barbara daisies and the occasional pansy, spills from a dresser drawer that now holds soil instead of socks.

On this exposed rooftop, where sun and wind can take their toll, mosaic pots that echo the furnishings and the hardscape can be moved into the shade as needed. Note the space-saving containers hung from the chimney in the background.

Container plants lining the route to an elevated deck make it look and feel like an integrated part of the lower space. Plants in similar colors under-score the connection.

If you're looking for large-scale containers, consider galvanized steel tanks. Not only are they affordable and available in a variety of shapes, but they can also serve as planters or ponds. Here, they contain an edible garden on a dining patio.

The owner of this garden incorporated everything, including the kitchen sink. A few well-placed dinner plates enhance the illusion of soap suds, which can be created with sweet alyssum.

One pot is nice, but several are better. These matching terra-cotta pots draw the eye along the length of a low wall.

Containers allow you to swap out plants without digging up an entire bed. Tired of looking at potted shrubs? Replace them with potted flowers. A pot holder cut into a bench can facilitate other quick switches.

An unusual container can highlight a plant the way this elegant pot turns purple petunias into a floral pompadour.

If a pot is intended as a permanent feature in a garden bed, it's wise to select one whose size and coloring corresponds with those of adjacent plants. The dark blue foliage cried out for a vessel like this one.

Repeated fountain
form unifies the
collection

garden notebook

grasses contained

The temptation with containers is to fill each pot with a

different flower to create a diverse mix of colorful plants.

But sometimes a well-defined collection connected by a common

thread results in a more calming statement.

  This group of choice grasses is clustered around a sitting

area. The grasses provide a changing display of flower heads

and fall colors, while being tough and pest resistant. They move

and whisper with each breeze, and they look equally dramatic

by day or when illuminated at night. The tones of gold and

blue-green work well with the varied colors and sizes of the

containers. The colors of the grasses themselves are also

balanced—the blue Leymus condensatus 'Canyon Prince' (far

right) is echoed by the low fescue to its left. A rampant

spreader like Leymus can be a thug in a small garden, but the

container keeps the grass neatly contained. If grasses are not

your thing, a collection of dwarf conifers or succulents can be

used in a similar way.

Dave

Taller pots highlight the weeping effect of the blades

Soft, evergreen foliage is kid- and pet-friendly

Refresh plants by dividing them every few years

Colorful containers take the place of fleeting flower color

potted paradise | a moveable feast of portable color

Clay pots that hold an assortment of cannas, gingers, and other cold-sensitive plants enjoy their moment in the sun on this intimate patio. But as soon as frosty winter weather arrives, they can be whisked away and relocated within the cozy confines of a backyard greenhouse.

Planted in containers, wispy grasses are dispatched in this multilevel garden anywhere their graceful foliage is desired. Here, they soften a few rustic steps and offer a counterpoint to the shiny finish on a pair of ornamental spheres.

A large pot makes it possible to bring the garden right up to the house. The vivid lime-green foliage echoes the color of a pair of wicker chairs set against the same bright blue wall.

Though this dining terrace receives full sun, its lush borders offset the stone floor
and invite you to linger in their cool embrace. The combination of leafy greens, as
well as red, yellow, and orange flowers, evokes a desert oasis where a glass-topped
table substitutes for a refreshing spring.

sun gardens

Some plants prefer to lurk in the shadows where it's dark and damp. But some—the sun worshipers of the garden world—like it hot. If you're wondering what to grow in a limited space exposed to blistering heat, start with the right plants and you've won half the battle.

Drought-tolerant plants make the savviest choices for full sun. Cactus is a no-brainer. So are succulents such as aloe, agave, and aeonium. Other good choices are santolina, artemisia, westringia, and other tough Mediterranean plants. Or go for the refreshing effect of bamboo and no-mow ornamental grasses, whose foliage gently rustles as it sways in the breeze.

On unprotected rooftops, containers with jade plant and echeveria need very little water. Flanking driveways, soft fountain grass and nandina won't scratch your car. Fences and trellises cry out for bougainvillea and trumpet vine. Whatever you plant, stagger the heights in layers— short in front, tall in back. Not only will you be able to see everything, but you'll also give shallow beds the illusion of greater depth.

Once you've got your plants in place, the next challenge is providing shade so you can enjoy your handiwork. A small tree in a corner or an airy hedge can cast dappled shade over your chaises or dining table. You can also take cover under a fade-resistant fabric umbrella or shade sail. Fixed awnings and pergolas are more traditional solutions.

The trend in indoor-outdoor living has made sun-blocking tents and patio drapery increasingly popular. While both can add stylish ambience, and even an ethnic flair, be careful not to seal off the overhead view. A small sun garden will seem infinitely larger and more inviting when you can glimpse the sky during the day as well as the stars at night.

Successive layers of cool-toned Japanese iris and hot-colored kangaroo paws act like magnets that pull the viewer toward a corner of the garden shaded by an umbrella.

While the green forms of cactus and succulents are silhouetted against the stark walls of this yard, a lone bougainvillea adds a jolt of lofty color.

A table, light sconces, and art combine with small palms to animate an empty wall. As the sun shifts throughout the day, so do the shadows, which impart a sense of movement and mystery to this outdoor room.

These cool-looking chaises and matching ottomans offer an inviting place to lounge outdoors, even on a warm summer's day. The furniture's airy weave carries over to the dark fence, and the chartreuse cushions pick up the color of surrounding plants. Containers help mask the expanse of bluestone hardscape.

Where blasting sun and water conservation conspire against a conventional lawn, a courtyard of decomposed granite and bluestone pavers means an end to turf wars. A place to sit and perimeter plants like lamb's ears prevent this garden from feeling like a neglected space.

A stepping-stone path is another alternative to a thirsty lawn. This one unfolds across a swath of gravel planted with drought-tolerant thyme that releases its fragrance when crushed.

Australian and Mediterranean plants can withstand mild, wet winters followed by hot, dry summers. Reliable performers requiring similar care are gathered in this vibrant border, including phormium (behind the stones), boxwood (in the pot), wallflower (behind the boxwood) and euphorbia, whose blue-green foliage and lime-green blooms are the border's centerpiece.

Various grasses, cacti, and succulents are placed along two garden paths so that their distinctive shapes and vibrant colors are backlit by the sun throughout the day. The euphorbia commonly known as 'Sticks on Fire' puts on a particularly dramatic show.

One way to design a garden is to combine plants with similar growth habits. Flanking this flagstone path are tufts of blue fescue and other ornamental grasses, each a different color but all able to tolerate bright sun.

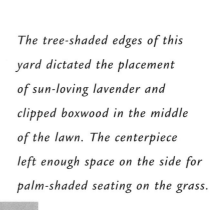

The tree-shaded edges of this yard dictated the placement of sun-loving lavender and clipped boxwood in the middle of the lawn. The centerpiece left enough space on the side for palm-shaded seating on the grass.

Brick planters organize plants in pleasing tiers that maximize a garden's available growing space. This type of vertical planting also allows you to segregate plants according to their water or maintenance needs.

dry style | compact oasis entertains all season

Where rainfall is limited, plant minimally, then play up a garden's other special qualities.
A stand of deciduous aspens shares this outdoor space in Santa Fe with custom amenities
such as a granite table, wood and metal stools, a black-bottomed spa, and a floor of river
rocks and stained concrete. The sleek handrail and wall sculpture serve as contemporary
but low-key accents.

The aspens are reflected on the polished surface of the dining table.
When their leaves drop in winter, the garden's walls of adobe and peeled
logs become more prominent, evoking a more traditional Southwest spirit.

garden notebook

sun-loving space

In small gardens, sun is a precious commodity that should not be wasted. The problem is that many avid gardeners cannot resist the urge to fill every last inch of their gardens with plants until they've produced a dark jungle of foliage. But in this sunny garden, the plantings fill all the available space while maintaining a feeling of openness. The mix of drought-tolerant perennials and grasses creates an informal meadow, while the garden's design makes the space seem larger.

In addition to being sun-loving, this garden produces an ever-changing tapestry of color and texture and requires a lot less work and water than a traditional lawn. The key is choosing low-growing plants of varying heights. As the plants spread and weave into each other, new and unexpected combinations of color and texture appear. Rising above this landscape, the redbud provides a tall accent without over-whelming the site or casting dense shade.

Dave

Olive jar becomes a simple sculpture

Lacy branches
don't block
the sun

Grasses and perennials
are a natural pairing

Plants are clustered
in groups for big impact

A mature tree has been pruned so just enough sunlight penetrates the canopy to support the shade plants in this entry garden. Together with the paneled facade of the house, the curved path through the moss and ferns calls to mind a secluded woodland retreat. Exposed roots complete the backwoods feel.

shade gardens

If your usable gardening area is located under mature trees, between neighboring houses, or beneath a stairway, chances are you're dealing with a small space with shady character. Not that there's anything wrong with that. On the contrary, during the dog days of summer, shade gardens can be rejuvenating places. But do keep in mind that areas with limited light require special consideration.

For one thing, many shade plants have dark green foliage—think ivy and fatsia. For variety's sake, include hosta, ligularia, or other plants with bright variegated leaves. While you're at it, try mixing textures such as strappy clivia with feathery ferns. For color, take your pick of blooms that range from ground-hugging impatiens and primroses to bushy camellias and hydrangeas.

Too much shade can feel cold and gloomy, so let the sun shine in by pruning a few branches from your trees and hedges. Or design fences with slats and walls with windowlike openings. Or add a fountain, pond, or mirror to make the most of reflections. By night, use low-voltage lights to cast intriguing shadows or hang a chandelier with candles for a little romance.

Shade often translates into moist conditions, so pay attention to paving. Paths of porous brick and decomposed granite absorb moisture like a sponge. The result? The growth of moss, which can leave you slipping and sliding. For safer, surer footing, install wood, concrete, stone, tile, or gravel.

When it comes to furnishing a shade garden, remember that iron rusts in high humidity. Powder-coated aluminum and most woods hold up better. Cushions are a double-edged sword. Once they get wet, they can be a magnet for mold. But keep them dry and—yep, you got it—you'll have it made in the shade.

Situated between two pergolas and a row of Italian cypress trees, this garden had to be designed for shade. Water-saving paving cuts a space-enhancing diagonal path.

By their very nature, shade gardens are damp places, so wood or plastic furniture often trumps wrought iron where upkeep is concerned. Plastic, shown here, requires zero maintenance, while wood may need the occasional resealing or repainting.

The light-colored exterior of this house offsets an assortment of dark green shade plants in a way that makes this corner seating area look warm and inviting rather than cold and dreary. A coat of paint can brighten masonry and siding.

Where shaded space is tight, make sure your walkway is kept clear and dry between waterings to prevent slipping. In the dark nooks and crannies of this garden, shrubs are clipped for a manicured look and white flowers function like footlights.

It would be difficult to maintain a healthy lawn in this tree-shaded backyard, so the owners opted for no maintenance at all. Brick paving unites paths and patios into one seamless whole. The patio's red edging encourages the eye to scan what lies ahead.

A giant vine-covered wall takes advantage of vertical growing space in this slender patio, where the ground is already planted chockablock with boxwood and hostas. Leaving the fence to the left bare keeps claustrophobia at bay.

A staircase laid out diagonally through this garden suggests
multiple levels and a larger space. Its living banisters consist
of trimmed boxwood and blooming mountain pieris that
appear to flow downhill like water.

Twin containers of Ficus benjamina *and symmetrical beds set the tone in this formal courtyard. Features making the space seem bigger are the gate and the walkway. These align with each other and share a geometric pattern that elongates their true dimensions.*

This nook sandwiched between buildings packs several space-expanding concepts into one diminutive garden: Fewer kinds of plants ensures a restful mood. Grow the plants at varying heights. Include a clear focal point. Link the indoors and outdoors.

Potted plants are a welcome mat that can change with the seasons. Here, a combination of Japanese forest grass, copper leaf plant, and coleus keeps the front porch looking fresh for visitors.

You can eke out more growing space around your house as long as you're reconciled to the existing light conditions, which may be dim. Here, the broad, ribbed leaves of hostas stretch out under a veil of climbing roses.

These densely packed beds of ferns and shade-loving bergenia convey a sense of cheerful abundance. The bright green foliage is a soft, cool counterpoint to the stone walk.

Groundcovers that hold up against light traffic can help take the hard out of hardscape. When allowed to fill seams along a narrow patio, they not only cushion the feet but are often accompanied by tiny seasonal blooms.

Not one but two rows of stone pavers surrounded by gravel and low-growing, low-maintenance greenery turn a side yard that's only a few feet wide into a user-friendly passageway. An umbrella serves as a focal point against a back fence.

garden notebook

backyard rain forest

A Costa Rican vacation might have inspired this garden, which is jam-packed with foliage to soften the hard edges of a truly tiny space. Instead of being preoccupied by the high walls that surround the garden, visitors to the welcoming space can wrap themselves in its lush display. As in a rain forest, where tropical plants with large leaves have adapted to the low light that filters through the forest's canopy, the big plants here appear to jostle for position. No single plant dominates; rather, they are layered one atop another to use every ray of light effectively. Tall tree ferns shelter masses of camellias, perennials, and lower ferns around their trunks. Splashes of color are provided by pots of campanula, lobelia, and trumpet lilies brought in at the peak of bloom. If your shady garden is in a colder climate, pair lacy Japanese maples with hostas, hellebores, and astilbe to create a quiet woodland setting.

Dave

Big leaves and
big shapes jostle

Vines draw
the eye up
and away
from walls

Pack in the
plants for
a lush look

Potted color blooms
with the seasons

Camellias provide color
in winter and spring

Marigolds—and lots of them—clearly star in this floral extravaganza; dahlias, morning glory, and hops play supporting roles. The lavish blooms demand attention in several areas at once, making the small space expand rather than shrink. The blue bistro table and chairs contrast with the hot-colored petals but echo the decorative tiles.

flower gardens

Flower lovers who plant nothing but roses or tulips are in for a rude awakening: Even the most magnificent blooms are here today and gone tomorrow. So if your heart is set on growing flowers in a confined space—where everything, including dormant plants, is up close and visible—factor the cycles of nature into your design.

One cure for seasonal shortages of flower power is an evergreen framework. It could be a hedge of boxwood, Indian hawthorn, or other shrubs. What matters is being able to count on luxuriant green foliage for year-round structure.

Another way around the problem is to combine several types of flowers for a never-ending parade of color. With research and planning, you can arrange it so that as one flower fades, another one blossoms, and so on in waves until each has enjoyed its 15 minutes of fame.

Perennials make the best, most economical flowers, since their blooms return year after year. If you want extra color, supplement them with seasonal annuals, either in the ground or in pots that can be changed as needed. Flowering vines can offer vertical pizzazz while hiding a blank wall or the neighbor's garage. Plants with interesting berries or leaf color can fill in gaps, too.

For a tranquil flower garden, limit your palette to one or just a few colors instead of a confetti-like jumble. A monochromatic, all-pastel, or all-hot-color theme will provide consistency and harmony. So will planting one kind of flower in dramatic sweeps.

In addition to looking good, many flowers also smell good. Grow the ones with enchanting fragrances—like gardenias and brugmansias—in and around favorite gathering spots. One whiff, and you're in paradise. Call it the original aromatherapy.

Red geraniums spice up a bland stucco wall. Displaying them in pots that drop into holes in the shelves protects them from being toppled by gusts.

An exuberant mix of flowers and foliage guarantees that passersby notice this streetside garden. The contrasting colors, textures, and shapes—from the dahlias and cannas to the dusty miller and pampas grass—combine to catch the eye and keep it entertained.

Roses high and low frame a statue placed prominently in the middle of the garden as a focal point. Note how the white stone gleams against the dark, leafy background but the black arch vanishes amid the climbing roses.

The bold yellow blooms of black-eyed Susan aren't for the shy and retiring, even when underplanted with more demure ageratum and sweet alyssum—they are more like a theater's spotlight. Honeysuckle, climbing amid the yellow flowers, will add fragrance.

A mix of red flowers and foliage pops out of this garden's greenery, which disappears into the shadows. When deciding on a color palette, keep in mind that stop signs are red for a reason, then proceed with caution.

Two rhododendrons of completely different hues don't usually add up to a balanced look. But judicious pruning, a quaint love seat, and color-coordinated pillows come together in one satisfying vignette.

When spring garden beds are chock-full, containers can extend the cavalcade of color. Here, pots of ranunculus, hyacinth, and daffodils brighten a modest patio. A container hung on the gate displays still more blooms.

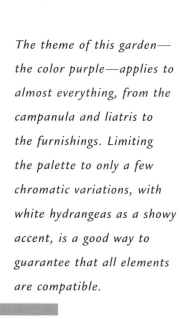

The theme of this garden—
the color purple—applies to
almost everything, from the
campanula and liatris to
the furnishings. Limiting
the palette to only a few
chromatic variations, with
white hydrangeas as a showy
accent, is a good way to
guarantee that all elements
are compatible.

Design your garden beds the
same way you'd snap a photo of
your family: Place the shortest
in front (thyme) and the tallest
in back ('Gertrude Jekyll' rose)
so that all can be seen. This
makes it important to know
the heights of your plants not
merely at planting time but as
they mature.

This clematis rambles along a rustic fence where, next to ruby red roses, its jewel-toned blooms double the flower quotient. For vertical color, train the vine on a trellis instead.

Tulips in rooftop planters provide spring cheer without the loss of ground space needed for building accessibility. While the flowers echo the red doors below, the box will weather and darken to match the old siding.

A hanging basket of trailing foliage or flowers like lobelia, impatiens, and pelargonium can give a shade garden a welcome shot of color at or above eye level.

The wisteria draping this arbor provides fragrance for the surrounding garden and masks an open-air wood shed beyond and below. When building a structure for wisteria, be sure to use strong, durable lumber— this one is made out of pressure-treated 4 × 4s and 2 × 6s.

brugmansia | two views of a signature bloom

Dozens of trumpet-shaped flowers dangle like pendants from this brugmansia, forming an enchanting screen between the house and courtyard. The blooms, often highly fragrant, are ideal for places where people are likely to linger and appreciate their scent: at a doorway, beside a bubbling fountain, or next to an open window.

Given the strong color of the home exterior, other plants hold their own without stealing the brugmansia's thunder. They include orange clock vine (climbing the front wall) and purple morning glory. Though not in bloom here, nasturtiums to the right of the gravel path bloom bright orange and yellow.

Lettuces sprout between limestone pavers, making it possible to pick salad greens just minutes before they're served on this Northern California patio. Chartreuse butter lettuce and bronze 'Red Oak Leaf' lettuce echo the existing aeoniums and phormium—and taste as good as they look.

edible gardens

If we are what we eat, then our vegetable beds should be, too. Sure, it's possible to be seduced by zucchini's gorgeous blossoms, even while detesting the long green squash. But if you grow only foods you like on your plate, you'll never waste valuable real estate on turnips or rutabagas again. While you're at it, you might even lower your grocery bills.

Homegrown crops can include carrots, onions, and other vegetables in conventional raised beds, the seeds sown closely together to maximize your harvest. But edibles such as beans, peas, berries, and grapes will take up less space when coaxed up a tepee, trellis, or pergola. Espaliered apples and lemons are happy against sunny fences or walls that absorb and retain heat.

Herbs and leaf lettuces, most conveniently placed a few steps from a kitchen or dining table, do well on their own or interplanted with vegetables. Plus there's no rule against mingling edibles and ornamentals, so why not tuck in a few colorful roses, cosmos, and dahlias to enjoy while crops get established or wind down?

Ensuring your produce is organic and chemical-free is a matter of green gardening. You can water properly and release beneficial insects to eliminate the need for harmful herbicides and pesticides. For nutrient-rich organic soil amendment, reserve a small spot for a compost heap of food scraps and garden clippings, or invest in an earthworm box.

Spring asparagus, summer tomatoes, autumn broccoli, winter beets—there's nothing like being able to have your garden and eat it, too.

A vegetable patch next to a clothesline harks back to a time when people raised their own cabbages and tomatoes. Here, beans and squash above white azaleas find breathing room atop twig tepees.

When cabbage exhausted the cultivable ground in this garden, other vegetables were trained to climb instead of sprawl. The fence offers extra support for trellises dripping with sweet peas. Next to the steps, even nasturtiums are encouraged to grow up rather than out. The design is efficient as well as attractive.

The hanging basket above contains the ingredients for a tossed salad—green and red leaf lettuce plus cherry tomatoes. The summer squash below dangles from a trellis like beans or tomatoes, maximizing space and reducing its susceptibility to mildew and disease.

Fruits and vegetables can be espaliered virtually anywhere in the garden. The wire trellis supporting this apple tree has a slim profile and footprint and therefore may function like a wall in defining the overall space.

Where horizontal space is a luxury or good drainage poses a problem, growing strawberries in a tall container like this one does the trick. It allows fruit to hang clear of wet soil but within easy reach as berries ripen.

Small pots of culinary herbs such as thyme, marjoram, chives, and rosemary are handy next to the indoor cooktop or outdoor grill. Keep them pinched back and corralled in a shallow tray, and they'll take up very little counter or shelf space.

This plot of lettuces is perfectly situated to save steps. Seeds are started in the greenhouse. Harvested greens are cleaned and dressed indoors. Finished salads are savored on the outdoor patio. And as plants mature, their ruffled leaves enhance views of the garden from every angle.

A basket of leaf lettuces augments the garden where the ground is reserved for edibles with different growing needs. The basket can be filled with fast-draining soil, watered as desired, and, of course, moved where the light is optimal.

Tomato fanciers with limited space are able to get their fix with cherry varieties placed in pots. The fruits may be small but many of them rival huge beefsteak tomatoes for flavor.

Practically every square inch is devoted to edibles in this terraced garden. Herbs spill over steps. Peppers bask in the sun in their beds. Squash matures in containers. And beans snake up posts and fences. Altogether, this is a prime example of wasting not and wanting not.

This raised planter in the middle of the garden provides deep soil, good drainage, and plenty of sun for a backyard corn crop. While the ears of corn come in, neighboring ornamentals such as zinnias, marigolds, and dusty miller bring visual interest to the space.

garden notebook

living with veggies

Instead of hiding vegetables and fruit trees away from the living areas of your garden, think of them as ornamentals, part of a tasty visual salad! This sunny patio plays host to pots brimming with colorful edibles such as cabbage, basil, and fennel. The planters are generously mixed with flowers to brighten the garden or dinner table. Unusual high-backed chairs echo shapes of bamboo tepees—and the chair in the foreground serves as a trellis for climbing peas and squash.

For your garden, consider tomatoes, especially heirloom types, which can produce sculptural, colorful fruits. Strawberries have attractive glossy leaves and bright white flowers. Even corn is ornamental, with its golden tassels and leaves striped pink or cream. Herbs such as golden sage, blue-flowered rosemary, silver thyme, and pink-flowering oregano are natural companions to annuals and perennials. And don't forget citrus, with its fragrant flowers and wintertime fruit.

Dave

Grapes provide shade, fruit, and fall color

Semidwarf fruit tree lends privacy

Pots contain living seasonal bouquets

Raised planters are easy to water and harvest

This Southern California backyard was envisioned as a place to unwind after sundown sans the typical lawn. It combines gravel, boulders, groundcovers, and ornamental grasses, and it comes with a seat wall wrapped around a firepit plus, a few yards away, a pond. The vintage surfboards offer clues to the owners' interests.

living spaces

Need more space? Planning to add on? Spare yourself the hassle and expense of a major remodel by treating your garden as another room, one with sky for a ceiling, earth for a floor, and plants for walls. You'll be amazed at how large your home turns out to be after all.

With alfresco entertaining the current rage, many people are installing fancy kitchens and dining areas outdoors. Built-in appliances and furnishings have undeniable custom appeal, of course, but a few words of caution: If you go for that big barbecue island, you'll be staring at all stainless steel, all the time. By contrast, a roll-away grill, a collapsible table, and a few folding chairs can easily make way for dancing or party games.

There are plenty of other ways to help your garden double as an open-air living room. Outdoor lighting makes a place functional and welcoming long after sundown. A fireplace, a fire bowl, or a radiant-heated patio or bench can provide comfort against the autumn and winter chill. An outdoor shower will work wonders for the body, and a meditation area will do even more for the soul.

Children and pets always need a small patch of lawn to play on. Where a jungle gym might not fit, there's bound to be room for a tetherball pole, a rope swing hung from a sturdy branch, or a stretch of walkway for hopscotch. Once toddlers have outgrown a sandbox, convert it into a vegetable bed or even a pond.

Remember to frame your outdoor rooms with plants to perfume the air or fruit to be plucked and eaten on the spot. But avoid anything poisonous or full of allergy-inducing pollen. And for areas around swimming pools, choose trees that minimize leaf litter so you can swim instead of skim.

Lanterns filled with votives and suspended from bamboo poles make this garden functional at night. The flickering light illuminates plants and objets d'art.

Just outside the living room of this house in Washington state, plants shelter a casual dining terrace. The floor and table base are fashioned from Chinese granite. Continuing the Asian-influenced design are slatted cedar screens along the breezeway and giant timber bamboo in the garden.

When night falls or the weather gets nippy, a toasty fire is both a practical luxury and a luxurious necessity. This firepit and built-in bench encourage hanging out in the garden, particularly for drinks or dessert. Marshmallows are optional.

Navigating this footpath in the dark would be a treacherous task, but thanks to a series of well-placed candles, the way is clear and trampled plants are a thing of the past.

Three destinations in this San Francisco backyard enlarge the space because each affords views of the other two. The lower patio is defined by bluestone flagstones and a stacked-stone wall. The pergola-topped bench is set off by granite pavers. And the hot tub is bordered by a redwood deck.

pebble power | gravel and pavers make room for plants

Smart multipurpose gardens like this one are good news for anyone who's married with kids and has very limited space. One central backyard area with a gravel floor functions as dining patio, tanning salon, and fireplace, all rolled into one. Furniture is light and airy-looking so as not to interfere with views. Extra seating is always available on the deck.

Concrete pavers lead the eye toward a burbling fountain tucked between ornamental grasses along the back fence. Note how shadows seen through the translucent panels coyly suggest that more garden awaits on the other side.

Even the tiny transition area between the driveway and yard here looks sharp. It features a grid of pavers seamed with woolly thyme. Orange-streaked phormium echoes the pebbles, seat cushions, and side table.

A dedicated storage space helps keep tools, potting supplies, and other garden essentials orderly, clean, and safe. Hang a plant outside and it can also make a rather nice place to rest between chores.

People who entertain often will appreciate a kitchen that blends into the garden. This one includes a sink, grill, and pizza oven with plenty of counter space for food prep and serving. Note how the stonework and plantings blur the lines between utilitarian space and landscape.

Grading turned a steep slope into this multilevel, multitasking backyard. The house now opens to a sitting area on the lower patio and a dining area on the upper patio. Between the two, a handsome stone retaining wall includes a fountain and orange-flowering plants.

A ladder and slide make a kid-friendly entrance and exit for a backyard playhouse. Note how, unlike primary-colored plastic play equipment, this wood structure blends into the landscape with the help of climbing vines.

Blackboard paint on a stucco wall creates space for children to express their inner Picasso. These chalk murals are an inexpensive way to bring art into the garden.

serious sideyard | a narrow space for work and play

With a little ingenuity, a sliver of a garden in Southern California goes from one nondescript passageway to three stylish outdoor rooms. A shower stands in for a bathroom, a seating area serves as a living room, and a sink functions like a utility room. The spaces are delineated only by vine-cloaked arches and subtle elevation changes in the cobblestone paving.

The wall-mounted sink provides a place to work without blocking the flow of traffic. It's made of limestone, the same material as the tiles on the outdoor shower. Creeping fig mimics green wainscoting and softens hard edges along the entire length of the garden.

garden notebook

versatile patio

Outdoor living spaces need not be complex. The centerpiece

of this garden is a simple patio that can be the setting for

a dinner party or a child's play area.

A low retaining wall contains an awkward slope, home to a

mass of plants that provides privacy from neighbors. A bench

that uses a section of the wall as its seat reduces the clutter

of patio furniture. Cafe chairs can be quickly removed to give

kids a place to play or accommodate a large party. Also taking

up very little space is the wall-mounted fountain, providing

soothing sounds while attracting songbirds. Vibrant paint on

the walls and bench cushions lend year-round color that plays

off the changing palette of flowers and foliage.

And the plants! There are lots of textures and shapes

here to keep a die-hard gardener like me interested. Some of

my favorites are the purple Cotinus and evergreen clematis,

which produces a bower of white flowers in winter.

Dave

Plants behind retaining walls are safe from pets and balls

Vines and wall decor take advantage of vertical spaces

Stone paving absorbs
then releases warmth
as night cools.

Winter bloomers, like hellebore, keep
the garden interesting all year

Though this graphic front walk is drought-tolerant, its smooth, gray beach pebbles were intended as a metaphor for water. Concrete pads were poured in place, then surrounded with the rocks so that each appears to float in a pool of stones. Blue-green senecio and red kangaroo paws grow nearby.

rock gardens

Maybe you live where it never rains. Maybe you consider water too precious to waste on irrigation. Or maybe you just like your gardens the way you like your martinis, neat and dry. If any or all of the above apply, there are plenty of ways to make a limited outdoor space a pleasure to gaze at and linger in.

The first and most obvious option is to take the desert theme and run with it. That means planting cactus, mulching with rocks, and laying out a path or two of decomposed granite. Cactus come in myriad shapes and sizes—some tall and rangy, others short and squat—but all are living sculpture that will soak up the sun and cast artful shadows against your "gallery" walls. Just give the plants lots of space to prevent any close encounters of the thorny kind.

Alternatively, plant azaleas and abutilons, then haul in a load of stones, and you've got the makings of an Asian-inflected vignette. With plants and small boulders punctuating an area of raked sand, it's possible to suggest a mountain range or a whole lake in the best Japanese tradition. Restraint, in palette and composition, is the key to a serene result.

By contrast, a Mediterranean landscape has a lusher look and feel. Dark green hedges combined with gray-green lavender, sage, and rosemary evoke the sights and heady scents of Tuscany and Provence. A gravel path that crunches underfoot and an olive tree for dappled shade complete the picture.

Whatever your garden style, going native—planting trees and shrubs that are indigenous to your part of the country—makes good sense for a host of reasons. Gardening with natives is always a water-wise move. Because they're acclimated to local conditions, native plants will need less water to become established. They'll also blend more seamlessly with the larger landscape beyond your home and thereby seem to expand the boundaries of your small garden.

This chunk of stone is large enough to serve as a bench next to a hydrangea. When not in use, it becomes a beautiful sculptural element.

Where lawn is swapped for a combination of gravel and large rocks, the result is less water needed for irrigation and a permeable groundcover that allows rain to soak into the earth.

Forget the fountain. Forget the green hedges. It's the gravel carpet in this courtyard that evokes a Mediterranean garden. While gravel makes an excellent surface to walk on, requiring only an occasional raking, it also serves as an effective mulch, retaining moisture and reducing weeds.

Ferns growing between boulders keep this retaining wall from overshadowing the adjacent path. Boulders across the path unify the split levels of the garden.

Reminiscent of ancient ruins, the stone walls in this yard make it look bigger by providing a staircase that wends past several garden beds. Trailing plants soften the expanse of mortared stone. Topiary spheres complement the curved walls.

Stones of myriad sizes, shapes, and colors form these whimsical floor and wall mosaics, which capture the zany spirit of the plantings.

new angles | multiple levels in a multipurpose garden

Like most backyards, this one is basically a long rectangle. But it stands out from the rest because of visually dynamic diagonal lines and elevation changes executed in various forms of stone. The space consists of a lower terrace of decomposed granite, a middle lawn, and an upper garden. Steps and seat walls of travertine and sandstone simultaneously connect and separate the different levels. Flagstone pavers leave room for plantings.

Different textures give the steps two distinct looks, depending on your vantage point. From above, the broad steps are smooth and precise; from below, their risers are chiseled and irregular. The vibrant blue accent wall presents another intriguing contrast. Its machine-made corrugated form is offset by the hand-hewn quality of the low planter wall in front of it.

Pots the same height as the seat walls preserve sight lines across the yard. In this way, trees and plants along either fence remain visible, enlarging the garden rather than diminishing it.

garden notebook

free-flow stonescape

In this rock garden, layers and levels of colored pebbles and beach stones create mulch for raised beds and a patio surface in one. Plants are not limited to defined beds but are scattered artistically across the surface, softening the hardscape's strong lines. Snakelike euphorbia and ball-flowered alliums will self-sow freely with the black foliage of Ophiopogon, which is spreading slowly across the gravel.

This is my favorite kind of garden, one where the plants are free to sprout here and there to suit their own needs, creating new and unexpected combinations. The open frame-work allows the gardener to experiment with thyme, aloe, penstemon, and other drought-tolerant perennials amid rocks of varying hues. The curving lines create visual movement while dividing the sloping site into shallow terraces that are easy to navigate on foot.

Dave

Wood sculptures add height without blocking sunlight

A multilayer fence disguises the back gate, making the space seem larger

The steel edge is modern but warm and blends well with gravel

Plants grow where the sun and soil suits them

Hollow log round becomes an eye-catching container

Thoughtful placement of a lap pool enlarges a space, especially when it's coupled with a raised planter running alongside. Between workouts, this lap pool doubles as a reflecting pond, mirroring the ribbon of tiles and chorus line of colorful plants above its glassy surface. The dwarf lotus in the pot in the foreground is one of several specimen plants.

water gardens

How can you introduce light, movement, music, privacy, and a sense of tranquility to a small garden? Just add water. Because no single element animates a space in so many ways, virtually all gardens—not merely those in hot, arid climates—stand to gain from water's soothing and life-affirming presence.

Eco-friendly recirculating fountains are the most common water elements, and no wonder. Whether they're custom built or bought off the shelf, freestanding or space-efficiently mounted on a wall, they bring visual and aural drama to the mix. Their flowing water masks unwanted ambient noise, creating privacy in a relaxed environment, while their beguiling falls and ripples glint in the sun.

To make the most of a fountain—or any water feature, for that matter—you'll want to place it near seating where you can see it, hear it, maybe even touch it. Classic locations are opposite windows, at the end of paths, or centered on a dining patio. Be careful not to put it where it obstructs traffic or poses a hazard to young children or pets.

If you prefer your water still rather than splashing, consider a fish pond. Although it may be placid on the surface, darting goldfish or carp can provide fascinating action below. A rill, a narrow rivulet only a few inches deep, is another understated possibility. It entices the eye along the length of its course, so provide a destination at the other end.

Finally, you can spike a reflecting pool with papyrus, lotus, or water lilies and use it to camouflage an adjacent spa. Or simply sit back and watch the water enlarge a space as it mirrors the vegetation around it and reflects the open sky.

The sedate character of this little corner owes much to the water spilling softly into its troughlike basin. The blue-green palette of the hostas in the low container is calming as well.

This naturalistic water garden is a visual treat for diners seated on an adjacent patio. Although cannas, lilies, and other aquatic plants may at first obscure the pond and the koi within it, the color of a bright orange Bauer oil jar blends in nicely when the fish eventually swim into view.

The simplicity of a galvanized steel tank goes hand in hand with this charming meadow garden. The tall pond remains visible amid the plush no-mow drifts of blue grama and mosquito grass.

A shallow fountain flows quietly into a pair of rills that bisect this lawn and stretch toward the far ends of the garden. By its very nature, a rill requires little space, making it a savvy choice for narrow confines.

Boulders and plants are so artfully arranged that this babbling brook appears to be nature's handiwork. Turn off the recirculating water, and the dry streambed is equally convincing.

A cast-concrete water sculpture by Oregon artist Tory Williams (below) and a stone floor fountain (right) incorporate moving water into the landscape in understated ways.

In this site-specific fountain, water dribbles down the sides of a ribbed vessel and into a rock-covered basin set directly below the pavement.

Pink water lilies in a blue container make it possible to enjoy a miniature Giverny up close. Pair them with pickerelweed for height.

From either direction along this brick path, the plant-filled pond beckons visitors to come closer for a better look. Once inside the space, they'll see blue pots anchoring the corners of an outdoor room and a decorative bench half hidden in the hedge that invites romantic tête-à-têtes or a few moments of solitude.

water landing | modern moat invites visitors

Just inside the front gate of this Southern California garden, visitors are greeted by the novel prospect of having to cross a lily pond to get to the front door. Fortunately, concrete stepping-stones, designed to look like thin slabs floating on the water, provide a safe, dry path. While dwarf bamboo marks the glass-paneled entrance, horsetail grows against a B-52 airplane wing that's been incorporated into the fence.

Concrete reappears in the backyard in the form of paving, raised planters, and seating. Red cushions and fence accents were chosen to amplify the tones of 'Lollo Rosso' lettuce, phormium, and cannas.

water way

Bigger is usually better when it comes to pots, sculptures, and fountains, but here several small components create one big idea. The water-washed sphere in the foreground, the small channel for water plants in the center, and the sculpture at the garden's left end create a path for the eye up and through the garden. Alone, each small feature would blend into the scenery, but together, in a limited space, they stand out. Everything is simple, with no fussy details or frills. I like that!

The channel is my favorite feature, its dark surface reflecting the sky and stars—a dwarf white water lily would be perfect there. I also like the way the elements cut through the different deck levels diagonal to the main axis of the garden. The wood and slate surfaces repeated from level to level provide variety, but not too much. As for the garden's lush background, here bigger is indeed better, as tall cordyline and perennials are used to blur the garden's boundary.

Dave

Elements
are aligned to
appear linked
from level
to level

Channel cut into deck appears larger and deeper than it really is

Golden foliage in pots leads guests up to a seating area

Simple lanterns highlight water features

Soft gurgle of fountain is soothing

Doors that open to the fresh air and skylights that filter the sun create a soothing indoor/outdoor retreat. Other details blur the difference between in and out: Pale blue paint suggests a swimming pool, white wicker conjures Grandma's front porch, and a lemon tree evokes a grove of citrus.

indoor gardens

Sometimes the great outdoors just isn't accessible—
in high-rise settings, say, or during bone-chilling winters. But this doesn't mean you're doomed to a gray,
plantless existence. A sunny spot in front of a window
or beneath an atrium can be parlayed into a kind
of miniature greenhouse. Yes, everything will have to
grow in built-in planters or portable pots, but the
logistical challenges are worth the dramatic boost
real foliage and flowers give otherwise lifeless rooms.

Natural light is key to a successful indoor garden,
so it's important to select houseplants suited to your
conditions. Good plants for bright areas include
dracaena, sansevieria, and kalanchoe; those able to
flourish in less light are spathiphyllum, coleus, and
aspidistra. Also worth considering are space-saving
hanging plants such as spider plant and ferns.
Popular during the 1960s and '70s, they're making
a comeback—sans the macramé slings, that is.

Humidity-loving African violets and orchids are
plants with a long tradition of indoor cultivation.
Meticulously pruned bonsai are also well adapted
for interior spaces. Display multiples, conservatory
style, in eye-catching containers, or arrange them on
special shelving. Either way, they'll become the highlight of any room.

And severely space-challenged green thumbs shouldn't
overlook that tiniest of all indoor gardens, the terrarium.
Under a glass dome or inside a widemouthed jar, Lilli-
putian landscapes of moss and ivy can be composed with
tweezers and chopsticks to sit on your coffee table, right
next to your copy of *Gulliver's Travels.*

*A sill just wide enough for a few cuttings produces
a kind of do-it-yourself stained-glass window.
Backlit colored bottles and vases produce brilliant
visual effects.*

Nesting tables provide a clever way to stagger the heights of your indoor plants. Here, white ones fade into the background, leaving foliage and flowers as the main attraction.

These potted herbs look like a well-planned part of the decor—good reason to buy containers of the same color, shape, or size.

Container plants of different sizes enliven this room and connect the interiors with the garden outside the window. The smallest anchor the coffee table, the largest doubles as a room divider, and the most colorful—pink orchids—really pop against the sunny yellow wall.

Orchids melt into the panoramic garden views in this sun-filled room, creating the feeling of being outdoors. Adding to the illusion are a row of orchids along the window and the terra-cotta pavers. Breezy white linens finish the look.

big concepts
maxing your space

scale ◎ shape ◎ verticality ◎ multipurpose design
color ◎ focal point ◎ texture ◎ pattern

scale

If you've ever tried to squeeze into a pair of old jeans, then you know that planting a mighty oak in a mini garden is just another form of denial. Far more practical is acknowledging the size of your space and scaling your plants, hardscape, and furnishings accordingly. Do this and, unlike Alice in Wonderland, you'll never find yourself teetering on a dinky chair or overshadowed by a gigantic tree.

When deciding what to grow, study your plants before you buy, to avoid overcrowding after they mature. Rather than constantly pruning full-size trees, train shrubs onto wood or metal standards and surround them with dwarf varieties of other plants. A half-dozen favorites will give you plenty of seasonal variety as well as the calm a small space needs.

In a well-proportioned garden, the biggest chunk of space should be devoted to your most important activity, whether it's outdoor dining, sunbathing, or gardening. Any remaining spaces can then be reserved for secondary purposes and linked so that they're seen at the end of a walk, up a few steps, or around the corner. The more you define your garden—even if the thresholds, paths, and multiple levels lead nowhere in particular—the larger it will seem, because it's impossible to overestimate the power of suggestion.

The principles of perspective worked for Renaissance artists; make them work for you, too. Lay out rows of trees, hedges, or columns along an exaggerated vanishing point. Or take two different plants with similar-looking foliage and place the one with larger leaves in front of the other to make the plant in back appear to be farther away. In either case, an optical illusion can be the next best thing to actually having more space.

This blank wall would have overwhelmed the garden if it had been left unplanted. But as a backdrop for a traveler's palm, its size and color are used to dramatic effect. Notice how the branches fan out in contrast.

Clusters of compact plants along a meandering path provide strong visual interest without ever obstructing a leisurely stroll through the garden. The single step up to a bench set in the rock wall creates a destination as well as the illusion of a larger space.

An elongated water feature follows the rectangular shape of this yard, inevitably drawing one's gaze toward the far end of the garden. The result is a heightened sense of distance that puts the narrow strips of lawn and the flowering borders into pleasing perspective.

Where full-size trees would eventually tower over this driveway and the parallel walk, 'Iceberg' roses pruned into standards serve as a low divider that's airy, attractive, and easy to maintain. To balance the cloud of white blooms, the roses have been underplanted with Spanish lavender and phormium.

Behind a comfortable love seat, an arched structure lends a feeling of enclosure without overpowering the scene. The open framework complements the slender trunks of nearby trees and keeps visible the surrounding greenery.

This sunken patio was designed primarily for enjoying meals alfresco, so the dining table was positioned in the big open space at the center. The patio and its low, lush plantings can be viewed from secondary areas of the garden, including the landing outside the French doors.

A visible place to sit beside a raised pond provides an inviting reason to walk outside and explore this garden. Because the path continues out of view both to the left and to the right, it suggests that there is more to the landscape beyond this tranquil vignette.

shape

Plants are the building blocks of a garden. That said, they're also its spheres, pyramids, cones, cylinders, barrels, and wedges. In other words, they're living objects with distinctive shapes, which in turn help shape their surrounding landscape.

Plants have predetermined growth habits, ranging from round to columnar, horizontal to vertical. Leave them to do their thing, or take out the pruning shears—topiary or bonsai, anyone?—to get the look you want. Related shapes echo one another and create a satisfying rhythm within an outdoor space. So you might accentuate a circular bed with boxwood globes or superimpose a rectangular myrtle frame on a rectangular lawn.

Other forms in the garden are ripe for manipulation, too. Consider the outline of your patio, pergola, borders, walkways, and pool as well as the contours of your furniture and accessories. Keep these shapes as similar as possible to underscore a theme, or vary them to produce interesting juxtapositions.

While straight lines and right angles convey human intervention and control, sinuous curves suggest nature's wilder allure. A straight path with a clearly visible beginning and end is clean and simple, but the lack of subtlety may seems to shrink a space. On the other hand, a meandering path, especially one that's partly obscured, has surprising seductive power, implying a larger space waiting to be explored.

Experiment with line and form, and as your garden starts to take shape, its character will follow.

The wavy outline of a mixed border offsets the straight fence line in the background and accentuates the natural fullness of the plants growing within. Rounding out the theme are soft mounds of colored foliage and the pom-pom flower heads of ornamental allium.

There's no denying the formality of a meticulously planned walled garden. Not only are the rectangular raised beds and stepping-stones laid out in perfect symmetry, but so are the two groups of Italian cypresses. As the only curvaceous element in the landscape, the oil jar stands out all the more.

The crisp right angles of this seat wall zigzag through the garden as a human-made counterpoint to nature's forms. The geometric lines are juxtaposed against plants with sprouting, trailing, or dangling foliage and flowers.

Circular logic—and a bit of whimsy—dictated the construction of a stone wall to complement the crescent-shaped canopy of this tree. Dark-colored slats that are nearly invisible span the void in the wall to keep the barrier functional.

Like a parade of beach balls rolling out to sea, these topiaries flank a path that gently wends its way to the house. The meticulously clipped globes form boundaries for other shrubs and trees that are permitted to grow more unrestrained.

On this modest terrace, tiles are embedded in the concrete in swirling motifs that call to mind flowing water. The vivid paving helps enlarge the space by focusing attention on the middle of the garden rather than on the perimeter. Note how the square cushions and pillows echo the tiles.

verticality

No room to spread out? Maybe it's time to grow up. Plants known for their tall, self-contained habits are perfect for limited space. Bamboo, horsetail, and snake plant—or even tree aloes or standard roses—also work well since they continue reaching skyward as they mature without growing bushy and encroaching on narrow paths or living areas.

You can achieve the same lofty goal by planting creeping fig at the base of a wall and letting it live up to its name. Before you know it, the wall's entire surface will be blanketed in green. Or you could coax a showy vine like clematis onto a fence and watch as it twines its way through the openings.

To reach new heights with other plants, you'll need to provide the support of an arch, arbor, pergola, trellis, or *tuteur*—the highfalutin French term for a garden obelisk. Even a minimalistic spiral of steel rebar may be all your jasmine, sweet peas, or climbing roses require to maximize unused air space.

Creatively combining flowering vines with tall evergreen hedges will reward you with a seasonal burst of color while still assuring privacy the rest of the year. Succulents or ferns planted chockablock through a vertical lattice can serve as a living green wall that's sure to be a conversation piece, and are easily maintained by a drip irrigation system.

Along side yards or behind buildings, you might consider a technique called espalier: Train your plants to grow flat against a wall, fence, or trellis by pruning their branches into decorative fan- or candelabra-like patterns. Apples and pears are the most common trees grown in this fashion, but lemons, pomegranates, figs, and avocados can work, too. Ornamentals such as crape myrtles, camellias, and dogwoods are other good choices for the upwardly mobile.

When no more ground space is available, plants encouraged to scramble across a wall will not only add greenery to your garden but cool it as well. Here, a prickly pear cactus is silhouetted against a wall that's come alive with the tracery of climbing vines.

The base of an outdoor staircase serves as a handy support for a flowering vine that reaches for the sun. A table and chairs tucked beneath the steps makes a shady secret garden out of what otherwise would be wasted space.

The showy orange flowers of Thunbergia alata *can turn a plain arch into a striking architectural element in the garden. The perennial vine produces blooms throughout the summer and is reliably evergreen the rest of the year.*

Years of patient pruning have paid off in the form of this garden's living pavilion of Sorbus aria *(a variety of mountain ash called whitebeam). Several trees were planted in a circle; then their trunks were carefully bent so the tops grew together into a leafy roof. Furnishings with equally graceful lines complete the backyard's look.*

There's no reason to confine your garden to ground level when a lattice arbor shrouded with climbing roses welcomes all who pass through it with glorious blossoms and intoxicating perfume. Choose a prolific bloomer, deadhead regularly, and be prepared for floral fireworks.

Taking advantage of sturdy eaves, a wisteria vine veils this house with thousands of fragrant white flowers. Containers and beds near the front door provide additional color before, during, and after the spring spectacle.

Almost any blank wall or fence, but especially one warmed by the sun, will make a hospitable spot for espaliered fruit trees. The branches can be grown flat in a variety of decorative designs.

garden notebook

wall rising

The walls of your garden don't have to be a flat plane.

This vertical garden is layered in tinted concrete planters

overflowing with succulents and a fragrant cascade of rose-

mary. Blue Senecio is a carpet under agaves; a tree aloe,

with tall flower spikes, attracts hummingbirds in winter.

No space is left unfilled, each plant working to create an

upwardly mobile picture. Clipped ficus in the background

provides leafy contrast and privacy.

    The elements that make this design so effective are

the bold shapes and colors, which are used here to disguise

the fact that this is actually a rather shallow space. In

a similarly shaped but shadier garden, try red bananas and

clusters of blue and yellow hostas over a carpet of purple

Labrador violet or ajuga. And instead of rosemary tumbling

over the wall, plant silver Lamium.

Dave

A variety of shapes keeps this garden exciting

Where access is tricky, choose plants that require little water or maintenance

Rosemary is fragrant and invites you to touch it when walking by

Saturated color livens up concrete walls

multipurpose design

It's the hard truth of a small garden: The less space you have, the less you can afford to dedicate any part of it to one activity alone. Designing a multifunctional garden is far more practical and makes you feel as though you've got more space at your disposal. It just takes a little ingenuity.

Say you like to cook and garden. Then by all means create an area where you can do both. When you entertain, a long tiled surface comes in handy as a buffet counter; when you garden, it doubles as a no-fuss potting bench. Likewise, a wide ledge with thick cushions serves as a daybed but also substitutes for chairs at mealtime.

A multitasking garden makes even more sense where custom amenities are concerned. Plan low walls around a planter or spa as informal party seating. Build an outdoor fireplace that works as a pizza oven. Use a foldaway table to cover a firepit by day. Choose a boxy bench with concealed storage for toys or gardening tools. Reserve spare cabinets around your barbecue for stowing everything from grilling gear to extra pots.

Plants can be multipurpose, too. Shrubs in the middle of a yard can divide it into separate areas while adding depth and color. Rooftop planters and hanging baskets frame views while providing shelter and privacy. The whole idea is to make your garden space as versatile as possible because the more ways you *can* use it, the more ways you *will* use it.

With space at a premium on this deck, custom walls and cabinets create several user-friendly options. Planters lift the garden to knee level and above, creating easy access for cultivation and maintenance. Built-in storage keeps a bicycle out of sight but within reach when it's needed.

In this small garden, the padded bench beside the dining table doubles as a daybed for the occasional post-lunch siesta. The wall, which screens out unwanted sights and sounds from next door, introduces a splash of Tuscan color and catches the shadow play of nearby palms.

This garden was designed to accommodate work and relaxation, with areas devoted to each activity in close proximity. A pair of Adirondack chairs looks out on a lively arrangement of container plants. Situated discreetly around the corner, a potting bench keeps tools and other gear organized.

Combine a miniature garden with a space-saving umbrella stand by retro-fitting a generous pot with an upright pipe anchored in concrete. Poking drainage holes in the wet concrete will allow plants to be irrigated without becoming waterlogged.

Tall hedges can subdivide a garden in a way that guarantees privacy and creates a pretty backdrop. A wall or a fence might have been just as serviceable for this intimate dining alcove, but neither would have matched the simple elegance of these green partitions.

An inexpensive way to brighten a dark corner is to hang a mirror that reflects light from sunnier parts of the garden. Here, not only does the looking glass remedy a black hole, but it also makes plants and flowers seem to stretch into an adjacent space.

focal point

One of the most powerful devices in your design toolbox is the focal point. Every garden needs one, to provide a visual anchor and set a tone. Just as you set a dining table with cheerful flowers or romantic candles, you can decorate a small garden with one or more elements to deflect attention away from those features that induce claustrophobia while spotlighting others that make the space appear more generous.

Almost anything can function as a focal point: A rare tree or specimen plant given pride of place at the center of a border. A fountain or statue situated at the end of an allée or tucked in an alcove. A birdbath or livestock trough used as a novel container. An outdoor fireplace or firepit that defines an outdoor living room.

A focal point can also serve its purpose by mere implication. Strategically placed mirrors, trompe l'oeil murals, faux windows, and false doors all suggest that there's more to a modest garden than a first glance suggests. They can seem to double the size of a space or create an air of mystery about what lies just beyond the bend.

Whatever they are, focal points should be unique and reflect your personality and your passions. If you're a collector, for example, displaying your prized seashells or watering cans or wind chimes where they'll be seen and appreciated will set your garden apart. Remember, a focal point is like a centerpiece—it's your chance to put your stamp on your garden.

A mirror strategically placed against a painted block wall bounces back an image of the garden in front of it and tricks casual observers into seeing another landscape through an open doorway. Note how the reflected garden appears to recede into the distance as though it were real.

Trompe l'oeil murals can leave visitors guessing whether the garden they're viewing is real or fake. Even an impressionistic painting like this one can fool the eye by artfully duplicating three-dimensional landscape elements—vines twining up side posts—in two dimensions.

A collection of birdhouses transforms a wall of shingle siding into a fanciful focal point. The fact that a birdhouse is normally nestled among plants in the garden makes this grouping all the more appropriate for displaying outdoors.

A salvaged gate can add exotic flair to a garden and look as though it's been in your yard forever when you coax ivy to grow through it and resist the urge to refinish it. A mirror completes the illusion.

A bold tile mosaic makes this path a much more interesting route through the garden than plain concrete. When planning all hardscape, think about how you can design functional features that are stylish as well.

This contemporary fountain's clean, spare profile is the
perfect foil for groundcovers laid out in simple fields of
color. A more ornate fixture would only have competed for
attention, detracting from the serenity of the small space.

There's no rule that says everything in a well-designed
garden has to be brand new. As this tattered wicker
armchair attests, many of the most charming elements
are vintage pieces. Here, petunias form a colorful seat
cushion.

color

When you design a small garden, it's not enough to say "I like blue" or "Pink is pretty." No, you've got to get in touch with your inner color theorist and analyze which colors do what and why.

Case in point: Light colors tend to recede from the eye, creating the illusion of greater distance. If you want to "enlarge" a garden bed, try placing lavender blooms—perhaps delphiniums or foxglove—toward the back. They'll take on the appearance of hazy objects seen on the horizon.

Bold, saturated colors, on the other hand, are attention-getters and hence space definers. Red poppies and orange cannas pack a strong visual punch. The same goes for dramatically dark colors such as burgundies, chocolate browns, inky blues, and purple-blacks.

When it comes to architectural elements and garden furnishings, the basics still apply. Lighter-colored walls or pillows—especially in nature-inspired shades of green or brown—fade into the background and allow your eye to focus on other things. Conversely, the darker they are—particularly in vibrant hues like orange or fuchsia—the more they'll stand out and make you conscious of the size of your surroundings.

Don't forget that all greens are not created equal. Plants come in gray-greens, blue-greens, and yellow-greens, plus bronzes, reds, and purples. Those boasting stripes, splotches, speckles, or spots are called variegated plants. Mixing leaves of different colors with variegated foliage creates the impression of a deeper garden.

A final note about the special qualities of white: It not only offers a crisp, clean contrast to greenery during the day, it also positively glows with reflected moonlight at night. Not surprisingly, it's a favorite in gardens big, little, and all sizes in between.

Sometimes greenery isn't actually green; it's purple or red. If not for the colors of the leaves in this border, it might not merit a second glance. But combining plants with different foliage palettes can lift a garden out of the ordinary.

Whether the red Kalanchoe orgyalis *along this ocher wall and walkway came first or the other way around, their warm colors evoke sunbaked afternoons. A few steps away, the green shrubs and blue wall conjure images of the same garden cooling off at midnight.*

This eye-popping patio consists of flaming orange walls and a cobalt-blue pergola. Injecting some of that vibrant color into the tropical landscape and around the small container lily pond are fiery variegated cannas flanked by variegated bamboo.

Bold leaves and flowers simulate backyard waterfalls, cascading from their raised planter toward the inky depths of a swimming pool. The splashes of chartreuse, red, and salmon keep the mood light around the dark-bottomed pool.

Fatsia, fern, spider plant, and turfgrass illustrate the broad array of greens planted in this garden. In the same small area, nemesia, a low wall, gravel, and concrete pavers contribute harmonious shades of blue.

Concentrating on one color can pay dividends. Unlike a rainbow mix of flowers, which would have been distracting, white tulips allow the eye to focus on the sculpture in the middle of this boxwood parterre.

Opuntia cactus and the succulent senecio share the same blue-gray tones and are therefore familiar bedfellows. Less common is pairing them with Japanese blood grass, whose tips look even more arresting next to the cool hues.

texture

A captivating garden is a many-textured thing. Nobody understood this better than the French artist Henri Rousseau, whose mysterious jungle scenes appear to fade to infinity thanks to layers of exotic tropical foliage. You can create depth-defying vignettes of your own by planting contrasting textures—lots of them.

Start with leaves. Look closely and you'll notice that they can be fine or bold, lacy or lobed, glossy or fuzzy. They can be needlelike, fanlike, round, oval, or oblong, with saw-toothed or scalloped edges. Zero in on flowers as well. Their delicate petals come in an array of forms: Besides stars, crosses, cups, and saucers, there are rosettes, trumpets, and pom-poms.

Trees contribute texture with their smooth or gnarled barks, while groundcovers range from tufts of grass to mounds of moss. With so many possibilities, it's easy to assemble a compelling mix. The goal is to make each plant stand out from the rest instead of letting it get lost in a monotonous blur.

The play of light off architectural surfaces presents other opportunities for textured contrast. Walls can be smooth- or rough-troweled stucco, plank siding, brick, or concrete block. Fences can be wrought iron, wood pickets, or translucent fiberglass. And don't forget the ground plane either. Loose pebbles, smooth limestone, precast concrete pavers, rustic flagstone, or wood decking—or some combination thereof—can each serve as a "rug" that pulls your outdoor room together.

Though texture doesn't leap to mind when you first start plotting a garden, it's one of the most useful ways to achieve the look you're after. The coarser or bolder the textures, the more casual—and smaller—the appearance of your space. Conversely, the smoother or finer they are, the more formal —and larger—the effect. The choices are entirely up to you.

Texture is ever-present in a garden; when placed so that they are viewed together, different textures can highlight one another. Here, coarse twigs woven into a rustic wattle fence contrast sharply with fine, carpetlike herbs growing on a bench below.

The various leaf shapes, sizes, and colors in this layered composition include hostas flanked on either side by lady's-mantle and crowned by a pagoda dogwood. Look for a diversity of foliage while shopping at the nursery to avoid predictable homogeneous clumps of green.

A path of loose gravel emphasizes the smooth concrete pads surrounding this swimming pool, and vice versa. The transition from one textured ground surface to another is a sensory experience, one that you can often see, hear, and feel.

The spiky white blooms of lupines soar over the low, spreading leaves of a creamy-edged hosta, providing a pleasing balance of form, color, and texture. Remove either plant, and the scene wouldn't be nearly as interesting.

One way to make a strong design statement is to gather plants in luxuriant drifts instead of stringing them out one by one. Here, chartreuse leaves stand out as important concentrations of color and texture amid darker foliage.

Set in the ground rather than atop a traditional pillar, this shiny gazing globe introduces light to the shadows beneath a pine bough and a low-growing Japanese maple. What's more, it focuses attention on the colorful glass mulch that might otherwise go unnoticed.

garden notebook

mixing it up

I like to play with plant combinations before I even dig a hole. Upon returning home from the nursery, I cluster the new arrivals in groups to get a feel for how they might look in the garden. I mix it up, contrasting green against gold or a tiny jagged leaf against a large round one. Think of it as pairing throw pillows on a sofa—a satin pillow looks great next to a tufted velvet one.

This gardener has chosen her plants carefully to make the most of a limited space. No boring plain green leaves here! Hostas, Heucheras, Rodgersia, and Hakonechloa grass combine for eye-popping results. Each leaf and color plays off the last, with a carpet of lime Alchemilla and golden ivy as a background. While each plant presents a rounded mound profile, the textures of the individual leaves and the strong contrasting colors help each plant stand out.

Dave

Grasses are perfect companions to perennials and shrubs

Don't be afraid of bold colors; here the combinations sizzle

Foliage color outlasts fleeting blooms in shady spots

Even a single specimen can enliven a dull expanse of ground cover

pattern

Most people prefer order to chaos, which is why pattern can work the same magic in a small garden as it does in a small room. Pattern not only organizes and ties disparate elements together but also is capable of making a limited space seem bigger. By stimulating visual interest somewhere within the garden, it distracts from the overall dimensions.

Repetition of shapes, colors, and textures forces the eye to recognize similarities. These visual cues frequently spell the difference between a garden that comes across as well-planned and polished and one that's a mishmash thrown together like a giant salad. One is hospitable; the other, haphazard.

Geometric patterns usually convey formality—think of a row of columns framing a portico, or a grid of pavers set into a lawn. More abstract patterns tend to feel loose and breezy—imagine plants with similar leaf shapes echoing one another, or a perennial border with its alternating masses of different colored foliage or flowers.

Virtually every surface or accessory—from ceramic tile and quarried stone to tableware and fabric for upholstery and awnings—can enliven a garden with stripes, dots, checks, plaids, paisleys, and more. When patterns from your interior decor recur in your garden, they help blur the distinction between indoors and out.

A garden of coleus and pelargonium makes the most of the plant's brilliant red and chartreuse coloration by packing the patterned foliage into a tiny area. The pointed leaves of one spill from an upper bed, while the round leaves of another crowd a lower bed.

Bricks in this tidy garden room are laid out in a classic herringbone to mimic an area rug or parquet flooring. Although the paving and home exterior are both masonry, the different patterns distinguish the vertical plane from the ground plane.

Once you've decided to let a vine run rampant across a wall, it takes only a regular pruning to transform it into a stunning conversation piece like this crisscrossed star jasmine.

The influence of Euclidean geometry is inescapable in this modernist garden. While square pavers frame one corner of the yard, long horizontal fencing encloses the opposite corner. The space in the middle is neatly divided between a rectangular patch of lawn and a rectangular walled courtyard.

A ring of saucer-shaped aeoniums alternates with other plants encircling a small citrus tree on this patio. Note that the round motif carries over to the shape of the pot and the shape of the tree's canopy.

Subtle patterns can be created by assembling seemingly disparate objects. Just as these square planting pots were set on square tiles set on a square bed, you could do the same with circles, triangles, and other shapes.

Don't be afraid to mix and match materials to come up with new and novel uses for them in the garden. Here, a whimsical checkerboard of green moss and blue glass makes a delightful transition from lawn to hardscape.

small wonders
plants and accessories

low to the ground ☺ midsize plants ☺ vines and climbers ☺ small trees
containers ☺ garden extras

This pathway garden demonstrates how only four types of plants can make even the most challenging small space look and feel large and lush. While vines sprawl over gateways and groundcovers pad the patches of dirt between pavers, midsize shrubs and small trees flesh out all the spaces in between.

what to grow

There are literally hundreds of thousands of plants you could choose for your garden, but when landscaping a modest area, you can simplify matters by zeroing in on a few dozen tried-and-true possibilities. Things get even easier if you think about plants in terms of the way they are organized here—that is, in four basic groups, sorted according to height and general placement in the garden.

Low-growing plants define the ground you walk on. These can be groundcovers only an inch or two high as well as slightly taller plants with either tuftlike or wide branching habits. Plant them alone as a substitute for a lawn, or combine them with paving or low walls to create a more solid stage for outdoor activities.

Medium-size shrubs function as the "bones" of a garden. You'll want to include some evergreens so that regardless of the season, your landscape never goes completely missing in action. Spotlight a handful of favorite perennials, too, and you can look forward to their spectacular flowers and foliage returning like old friends from year to year.

Vines are indispensable space-saving plants since they grow where others can't. While their high-climbing leaves and blooming color allow you to hide unattractive features such as bare walls and chain-link fences, they also enable you to accentuate lofty pergolas, regal balustrades, and other elements.

Small trees form the upper boundary of the garden. Since full-size trees require constant pruning to keep them in proportion to tight spaces, it's wise to plant dwarf varieties—in some small gardens, large shrubs are large enough. Besides saving you a lot of work, small trees are instrumental in framing views, providing shade, and serving as natural focal points.

low to the ground

midsize plants

vines and climbers

small trees

periwinkle

vinca major

Lavender-blue flowers in spring; arching habit; can be invasive; good under trees with leaf litter.

1–2 feet high
☼ ◑ ● full sun in cooler climates only
◊ ◖ little to moderate water

santa barbara daisy

erigeron karvinskianus

Dainty pink and white blooms from spring to summer; mounding habit; drought-tolerant; use in mixed borders.

10–20 inches high
☼ ◑ full sun or light shade
◖ moderate water

golden star

chrysogonum virginianum

Yellow star-shaped flowers in spring and fall; spreading habit; good filler in woodland settings.

10 inches high
☼ ◑ sun or partial shade
◖ regular water

(caption on left margin, vertical text) low to the ground

salal

gaultheria shallon

Glossy round leaves; grow in rock gardens, woodland settings, and with acid-loving plants; drought-tolerant.

4–10 feet high
◑ partial shade
◖ regular water

carpet bugle

ajuga reptans 'Catlin's Giant'

Dazzling blue flower spikes from spring to early summer; good filler but can be invasive.

8 inches high
☼ ◑ full sun or partial shade
◖ regular water

cranesbill

geranium sanguineum

Long-lasting blooms; lobed leaves; attractive in rock gardens; small varieties include 'Album' and 'Max Frei'.

1–1½ feet high
☼ ◑ afternoon shade in hottest climates
◖ regular water

blue fescue
festuca glauca

Tufts of fine blue-gray to silver leaves; use in geometric patterns as edging or as a groundcover.

1 foot high
☀️◑ best in sun, tolerate some shade
💧💧 moderate to regular water

japanese forest grass
hakonechloa macra 'Aureola'

Green leaves with yellow to chartreuse stripes; arching habit; good in shade gardens and containers.

14 inches high
☀️◑● full sun in cooler climates only
💧 regular water

plantain lily
hosta 'Blue Cadet'

Blue-green heart-shaped leaves; plant in borders with early-spring bulbs and ferns; susceptible to slugs and deer.

15 inches to 3 feet high
◑● partial or full shade
💧 regular water

echeveria
echeveria agavoides

Fleshy rosettes of green leaves with reddish brown tips; good in rock gardens and indoors.

6 inches high
☀️◑ full sun or partial shade
💧 regular water

lady's-mantle
alchemilla mollis 'Auslee'

Long-lasting greenish yellow sprays of flowers from summer to fall; velvety cupped leaves; great in masses.

2 feet or higher
☀️◑ full sun in cooler climates only
💧 regular water

heartleaf bergenia
bergenia cordifolia

Glossy evergreen leaves with wavy edges; lilac flower clusters; ideal in woodland borders and under trees.

1½ foot high
◑● partial or full shade
💧 regular water

summersweet
clethra alnifolia

Fragrant white or pink flower spikes; dark green toothed leaves; attracts beneficial insects; good by streams.

4–10 feet high
☼ ◑ best in partial shade but adaptable
◖ regular water

camellia
camellia japonica

White, pink, or red flowers; glossy evergreen leaves; compact varieties include 'Finlandia' and 'Kramer's Supreme'.

6–12 feet high
◑ ● best out of strong sun
◖ ◖ moderate to regular water

lily-of-the-valley shrub
pieris japonica

Fragrant white, pink, or red flower clusters; glossy evergreen leaves; combine with azaleas in woodland settings.

9–10 feet high
◑ filtered sunlight or partial shade
◖ regular water

bridal wreath spiraea
spiraea prunifolia 'Plena'

Tiny white blooms on bare branches in spring and summer; arching habit; handsome against hedges.

6–7 feet high
☼ ◑ full sun or light shade
◖ ◖ moderate to regular water

bigleaf hydrangea
hydrangea macrophylla

White, pink, or blue flowers; large toothed leaves; use in borders and dried arrangements.

4–8 feet high
☼ ◑ partial shade in hottest climates
◖ regular water

mexican bush sage
salvia leucantha

Velvety white and purple blooms; aromatic gray-green leaves; drought-tolerant; attracts hummingbirds.

3–4 feet high
☼ full sun
◖ regular water

forsythia

forsythia × intermedia 'Lynwood'

Tawny yellow blooms precede leaves in spring; ideal as screen or espalier or in shrub border.

7 feet high

☼ full sun

◑◑ moderate to regular water

delphinium

delphinium

Blue, white, red, pink, or purple spires; lobed leaves; good in borders and containers; attracts birds.

1–8 feet high

☼ full sun

◑ regular water

canna

canna 'Bengal Tiger'

Orange flowers; large green and yellow striped leaves; grow in borders, near ponds, and in pots.

4–6 feet high

☼ full sun

◑ regular water during growth and bloom

cape plumbago

plumbago auriculata 'Royal Cape'

Brilliant blue flower clusters nearly year-round; evergreen leaves; mounding habit; great filler for large area.

6 feet high

☼◑ full sun or light shade

◌◑◑ little to regular water

horsetail

equisetum hyemale

Upright green hollow stems with dark banded joints; invasive and best in containers; good as screen.

6 inches to 4 feet high

☼◑ full sun or partial shade

◑◑ locate in marshy area or pond

fountain grass

pennisetum setaceum 'Rubrum'

Reddish brown leaves; furry pink flower plumes; arching habit; great as color accent and for movement.

5 feet high

☼◑ full sun or partial shade

◑◑ moderate to regular water

creeping fig
ficus pumila

Softens walls with delicate evergreen tracery when young and leathery leaves when mature; can be invasive.

climbs by attaching rootlets
☼ ◐ ● sun or shade
💧 regular water

trumpet creeper
campsis radicans

Scarlet trumpet-shaped flowers in summer; glossy leaves; good as fast-growing screen; can be invasive.

climbs by attaching rootlets
☼ ◐ ● full sun or partial shade
💧💧 moderate to regular water

mandevilla
mandevilla × amoena 'Alice du Pont'

Pink funnel-shaped flowers from spring to fall; evergreen leaves; needs pergola, trellis, or stake for support.

climbs by twining stems
☼ ◐ full sun or partial shade
💧 regular water

virginia creeper
parthenocissus quinquefolia

Green leaves turn red in fall followed by black berries; makes clever camouflage; can be invasive.

climbs by suction discs on tendrils
☼ ◐ ● sun or shade
💧 moderate water

lilac vine
hardenbergia violacea 'Happy Wanderer'

Pinkish purple blooms in winter and early spring; trailing habit; needs support; grow on trellises.

climbs by twining stems
☼ ◐ partial shade in hottest climates
💧 moderate water

hop
humulus lupulus 'Sunbeam'

Large chartreuse leaves; small cone-shaped and pine-scented flowers in late summer; good as screening device.

climbs by twining stems
☼ full sun
💧 regular water

carolina jessamine

gelsemium sempervivens

Fragrant yellow blooms; trailing habit; great on trellises, walls, fences, and mailboxes; poisonous if ingested.

climbs by twining stems
☼ ◑ full sun or partial shade
◉ regular water

nasturtium

tropaeolum

Edible red, yellow, and orange flowers and round leaves have peppery flavor; plant in vegetable gardens.

climbs by coiling leafstalks
☼ ◑ full sun or light shade
◉ regular water

clematis

clematis

Wide range of showy flowers; needs trellis or tree trunk for support; *Clematis* × *jackmanii* is popular.

climbs by curling leafstalks
☼ roots cool, top in sun
◉ regular water

scarlet trumpet honeysuckle

lonicera × *brownii* 'Dropmore Scarlet'

Unscented red tubular blooms followed by red berries; attracts hummingbirds; ideal on trellises, fences, and gates.

climbs by twining stems
☼ ◑ full sun or partial shade
◉◉ moderate to regular water

grape

vitis vinifera 'Perlette'

Provides yellow seedless fruit and shade; grow on trellis, arbor, fence, or wire; spur pruning recommended.

climbs by tendrils
☼ full sun
◉ moderate water

rose

rosa

Wide range of lavish blooms; train on arbors and fences; natural climbers include 'Eden' and 'Joseph's Coat'.

climbs by being tied to support
☼ ◑ full sun or light shade
◉ regular water

witch hazel

hamamelis mollis

Green leaves turn yellow in fall; fragrant yellow flowers on bare stems in winter; spreading habit.

8–30 feet high
☼ ◗ full sun or partial shade
◖ regular water

eastern redbud

cercis canadensis

Pink, purple, or white flowers on bare branches in spring, followed by bean-like pods; fastest-growing redbud.

25–35 feet high
☼ ◗ full sun or light shade
◖◖ moderate to regular water

crape myrtle

lagerstroemia indica 'Natchez'

Profusion of white flowers in summer; orange-red leaves in fall; handsome peeling bark; very disease-resistant.

25 feet high
☼ full sun
◖ moderate water

smoke tree

cotinus coggygria 'Royal Purple'

Named after fuzzy lavender-pink hairs following faded green blooms; purple leaves from spring to fall; multitrunked.

12–15 feet high
☼ full sun
◖ moderate water

river birch

betula nigra

Prized for peeling bark; tiny diamond-shaped leaves; multitrunked; small varieties include 'Little King'.

10–12 feet high (small varieties only)
☼ full sun
◖ regular water

japanese maple

acer palmatum

Lobed green leaves turn scarlet, orange, or yellow in fall; good for patios and woodland settings.

20 feet high
☼ ◗ full sun or partial shade
◖◖ moderate to regular water

apple

rosaceae

Valued for fruit; dwarf and semidwarf trees can be espaliered; multiple varieties available on one tree.

5–8 feet high
☼ full sun
💧 regular water during fruit development

chaste tree

vitex agnus-castus

Fragrant lavender-blue flower spikes; aromatic gray-green leaves; multitrunked; grows quickly; works as tree or shrub.

25 feet high
☼ full sun
💧💧 moderate to regular water

banana

musa

Broad evergreen leaves sometimes variegated; dwarf varieties ideal near pools and in tropical settings.

7–15 feet high
☼ full sun
💧 ample water

lemon

citrus limon

Valued for fruit; fragrant white flowers; glossy leaves; does not require high heat; good in pots.

6–22 feet high
☼ full sun or bright light
💧 regular water

bamboo

bambusa multiplex

Clumping variety but root barrier suggested; fountainlike habit; use as clipped hedge or unclipped natural screen.

8–10 feet when drier, 15–25 feet when wetter
☼ ◑ sun or partial shade
💧💧💧 little to regular water

pygmy date palm

phoenix roebelenii

Feathery green leaves; good for driveways, by pools, and in pots; single- or multitrunked.

6–10 feet high
☼ ◑ full sun or partial shade
💧 regular water

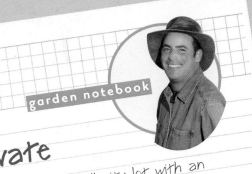

garden notebook

Public and private

Here is a common situation: a small city lot with an abrupt grade change from street to house, and not a lot of room for a garden. Instead of throwing up their hands, the owners of this home got creative and moved their garden out onto the street. First came a low stone retaining wall, now crowned with a leafy wall of ceanothus and flowering shrubs.

Then they tackled the hell strip—that no-man's-land between the curb and the sidewalk that's typically planted in trampled grass. Here the strip sports tough Mediterranean plants that thrive in the reflected heat and poor soil. The strip overflows with Kniphofia, catmint, Stipa, and Verbascum. Penstemon, Achillea, Gaillardia, and verbena provide lots of color but can take the occasional errant dog or careless footstep. The space is totally public, but still reflects the tastes and ideas of the homeowners.

Dave

Gravel mulch holds moisture

Tall plants provide leafy privacy for street-facing windows

Fragrant foliage releases its scent as pedestrians brush by

Pebble mosaic allows access from the street

Plantings are low enough to provide a clear view for safety

containers

Wall-mounted window boxes create gardens even where space is very limited. Filled with a combination of upright and trailing plants, a window box can enhance your home's exterior facade as well as improve the view from indoors. An attractive frame with a removable liner makes for easy seasonal changes.

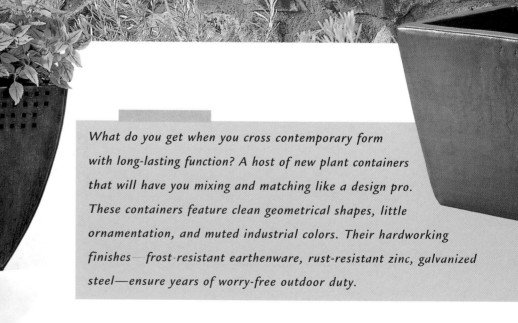

What do you get when you cross contemporary form with long-lasting function? A host of new plant containers that will have you mixing and matching like a design pro. These containers feature clean geometrical shapes, little ornamentation, and muted industrial colors. Their hardworking finishes—frost-resistant earthenware, rust-resistant zinc, galvanized steel—ensure years of worry-free outdoor duty.

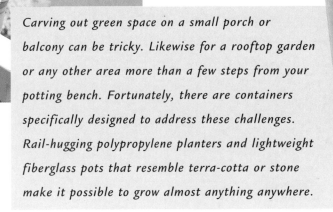

Carving out green space on a small porch or balcony can be tricky. Likewise for a rooftop garden or any other area more than a few steps from your potting bench. Fortunately, there are containers specifically designed to address these challenges. Rail-hugging polypropylene planters and lightweight fiberglass pots that resemble terra-cotta or stone make it possible to grow almost anything anywhere.

If you need a place to sit and garden, consider a dual-purpose planter bench like this one. The long seat comes in handy for informal gatherings, while the deep containers at either end accommodate flowers and even small trees. More seats and containers can be added as needed.

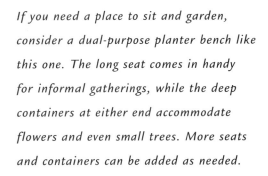

garden extras

Wall fountains bring water's entrancing sight and sound to small gardens without sacrificing precious space that could be cultivated. Many are designed for the do-it-yourselfer, which means they're made of easy-to-hang lightweight fiberglass and come equipped with recirculating water pumps that plug into any standard outlet.

A storage bench gives you an attractive spot to stash gardening tools before party guests arrive. Such multipurpose benches, available in various sizes, can be fashioned from cedar and other insect-resistant materials and be covered with waterproof cushions and covers.

Arbors make charming focal points against a wall or fence, framing a seat or suggesting a threshold to another space. Models made of vinyl-coated galvanized steel are sturdy enough to support climbing vines and withstand the elements.

To reduce the need for electricity and to lower utility bills, more and more environmentally conscious gardeners are turning to solar-powered fountains. These self-contained "green" water elements depend on solar panels to harness sunlight that is then converted to energy and used to operate a recirculating water pump.

Fountains of granite and other stone that has been carved into spare sculptural forms look simultaneously Eastern and Western, ancient as well as modern. A stone fountain can be used alone as a bold centerpiece or tucked among plants as a more subtle visual surprise.

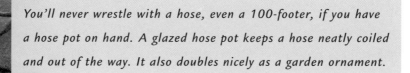

You'll never wrestle with a hose, even a 100-footer, if you have a hose pot on hand. A glazed hose pot keeps a hose neatly coiled and out of the way. It also doubles nicely as a garden ornament.

design credits

front matter cover *Garden design:* Judy Horton; *Chair design:* Suzanne Rheinstein and Associates **1** Manolo Vega **2 left** Raul Zumba, Zumba Gardens **3 bottom left** Smith & Hawken **3 bottom right** Lisa Ray **5** DCA Landscape Architects **7 bottom right** Rob Steiner Gardens, robsteinergardens.com

big ideas|garden by garden **8 top** Nick Williams & Associates, nickwilliamsdesigns.com **9** Shari Bashin-Sullivan **12** Susan Slater **13 top right** M&M Nursery **13 bottom** Anthony Paul Design **14 left** M&M Nursery **15 top left** Dan Pearson **15 bottom** Philip Watson **17** Geoffrey Whiten **18–19** Diana Strattom **20** Shari Bashin-Sullivan **21** Merilee Kuhlmann, Comfort Zone Garden Design **22 bottom** Sam Woodruff and George Fischer **23** *Garden design:* Judy Horton; *Chair design:* Suzanne Rheinstein and Associates **24 left** Merilee Kuhlmann, Comfort Zone Garden Design **26 bottom right** Kat Sawyer **28–29** Clemens & Associates **31** Corrado Giovannoni Design **33** Linda Engstrom **34 left** Tom Mannion **34–35** Annie Wilkes **35 right** Clinton & Associates **36–37 bottom** Yunghi Choi **39 left** Bud Stuckey **39 right** Alvaro Ponce **40 top right** Church Hill Cottage **43** Kim Whodmore **45** Dan Pearson **47 bottom** Swinton Lane **52** Rob Steiner Gardens, robsteinergardens.com **54** Raul Zumba, Zumba Gardens **56** Chelsea 2001, Stone Market Garden **60 top left** Chelsea 02, Aylesbury College **63** Kate Frey **64** Nick Williams & Associates, nickwilliamsdesigns.com **66 bottom** Green Scene Landscape Design **67 bottom** Terry Mulrooney, Admiral Green Landscaping, admiralgreen.com **68–69** Rob Steiner Gardens, robsteinergardens.com **70 top** Cherry Burton **71 top left** Elliot Goliger, Artisans Landscape, artisanslandscape.com **71 bottom right** Jeffrey Miller, ASLA Miller Company Landscape Architects, millercomp.com **72–73** Theresa Clark **75** Corrado Giovannoni Design **77** vermeilDesign, vermeildesign.com **78 left** EPT Design **78 right** Rob Steiner Gardens, robsteinergardens.com **79 bottom left** Judith Glover **80–81** vermeilDesign, vermeildesign.com **83** Alison Wear & Miranda Melville **86** Rob Steiner Gardens, robsteiner gardens.com **87 bottom** Brad Stangeland **88 left** Nick Williams & Associates, nickwilliamsdesigns.com; *Fountain:* Tory Williams **93** Kristina Fitzsimmons, June London **96 left** Ellen Spector Platt

big concepts|maxing your space **98 bottom** Debra Burnette **99** Freeland Tanner, Proscape Landscape Design **100** Manolo Vega **101 left** Cheryl Waller **101 right** John Plummer **102 top** Freeland Tanner, Proscape Landscape Design **102 bottom** Laurie Callaway Garden Design, callawaygardendesign.com **103 top** Kat Sawyer **104** Margaret de Haas van Dorsser **105 bottom** Shelly Marsterson **106 top** Maggie Judycki **106 bottom** Philip Watson **107** Flower to the People, flower2people.com **108** Dan Overbeck **109 right** Flower to the People, flower2people.com **115 bottom** Lucy Hardiman **117 right** Mike Catherine & Raymond Beard **119 bottom** Linda Terhark **121 right** Julie Moir Messervy **122** B. Smith &

D. Schrader **123 top** Debra Burnette **123 bottom** Lisa Ray **124 top right** Tom Mannion **126** Yvonne Mathews **127** C. Woodhouse **128 right** Allison Armour-Wilson **129 top** Timothy Vaughan **133 top** Maggie Judycki **134** Bernard Trainor Design **135 top right** Jeff Powers **135 bottom right** Claire Whitehouse

small wonders|plants and accessories **137** Smith & Hawken **140 bottom center and 142 bottom left** Connie Cross **143 top right** Lisa Ray **148 left and 149** Lucy Hardiman **150 top right and bottom left** Smith & Hawken **150 bottom right** Ikea **151 top left** Gardeners.com **151 top right** Smith & Hawken **151 bottom left** Ikea **151 bottom right** Iron Hand Crafts, unicahome.com **152 left** GardenArtisans.com **152 top right** Garden-Fountains.com **152 bottom right** CleanAirGardening.com **153 center, top right, and bottom right** KineticFountains.com **153 bottom left** Smith & Hawken

photography credits

courtesy **Big Sur Media, Inc.:** 16, 30, 42, 62, 74, 82, 92, 112, 130, 148; **Mark Bolton/The Garden Picture Library:** 67 top; **Marion Brenner:** 3 bottom right, 71 top left, 79 right, 99, 102 top, 123 bottom, 128 left, 134, 136 bottom, 141 bottom left, 143 top right, 147 top right; **Rob D. Brodman:** 57, 67 bottom; **David Cavagnaro:** 70 bottom, 111 bottom, 132, 140 top left, 141 top right, 142 bottom left, 143 bottom right, 145 bottom left; **Van Chaplin/SPC:** 146 bottom center; courtesy **Clean AirGardening.com:** 152 bottom right; **Jack Coyier:** 76, 78 left; **Rosalind Creasy:** 44, 48 bottom, 58, 60 bottom, 60–61 top; **Claire Curran:** 13 top right, 14 left, 15 top right, 97, 109 left, 110–111 bottom, 133 bottom, 135 top right; **Robin Bachtler Cushman:** 140 bottom left and bottom right, 144 bottom left, 146 top left; **Arnaud Descat/M.A.P.:** 98 top, 129 top, 131; **Alan & Linda Detrick:** 36 top, 47 top right, 96 left, 126, 144 top right, 145 bottom right; **F. Didillon/M.A.P.:** 40 top right; **Linda Enger:** 98 bottom, 123 top; **Catriona Tudor Erler:** 84, 88 right, 95, 105 top, 110 left, 120 top, 128 right; **Ron Evans/The Garden Picture Library:** 145 top right; **Roger Foley:** 5, 15 bottom, 32, 34, 35 right, 36–37 bottom, 103 bottom, 106 top, 106 bottom, 124 top right, 133 top, 146 top right; courtesy **GardenArtisans.com:** 152 left; courtesy **Gardeners.com:** 151 top left; courtesy **Garden-Fountains.com:** 152 top right; **Suzie Gibbons/The Garden Picture Library:** 94; **John Glover/The Garden Picture Library:** 7 left, 17, 45, 51 right, 57, 93; **David Goldberg/Susan A. Roth & Co.:** 59 bottom left, 93 all, 147 bottom left; **Juliet Greene/The Garden Picture Library:** 70 top; **Steven Gunther:** 8 top, 53, 64 top, 72–73, 88 left, 90–91, 107, 113, 118, 139 bottom, 147 bottom right; **Gil Hanly/The Garden Picture Library:** 38; **Lucy Hardiman:** 148 left, 149; **Lynne Harrison:** 145 top left; **Saxon Holt:** 2, 9, 18, 19 all, 20, 24–25 top, 54, 87 top left, 140 top center, 141 top left, 143 bottom center, 145 bottom center; **Michael Howes/The Garden Picture Library:** 65; courtesy **Ikea:** 150 bottom right,

151 bottom left; **Dency Kane:** 142 bottom right; **courtesy KineticFountains. com:** 153 center, top right, and bottom right; **Dennis Krukowski:** 4, 13 top left; **Melba Levick:** 3 top, 26 top, 27 bottom, 37, 61 bottom, 111 top, 115 top, 116 top right; **Janet Loughrey Photography:** 25 right, 46, 48 top, 51 left, 89, 104, 115 bottom; **Allan Mandell:** 33, 41 left, 119 bottom, 121 right, 141 top center; **Charles Mann:** 147 top center; **Jeffrey Miller:** 71 bottom right; **Nicole & Patrick Mioulane/M.A.P.:** 55; **Clive Nichols/ M.A.P.:** 2 top right, 6 bottom, 47 bottom, 56, 60, 66 top right, 85, 122, 127; **Jerry Pavia:** 22 top, 40 bottom left, 47 top left, 119 top, 121 left, 125 bottom, 136 top, 141 bottom center, 141 bottom right, 143 top center, 144 top left; **Norm Plate:** 14 top right, 28–29 all, 41 right, 108; **Lisa Romerein:** 7 right, 10, 52, 68–69 all, 71 bottom left, 78 right, 86, 138, 147 bottom center, 155; **Susan A. Roth:** 139 top and second from top, 140 top right and bottom center, 142 top left, top right, and bottom center, 143 top left and bottom left, 144 top center and bottom right; **Richard Shiell:** 139 second from bottom, 142 top center, 144 bottom center; **John Ferro Sims/The Garden Picture Library:** 6 top; **J. S. Sira/The Garden Picture Library:** 43, 87 top right, 120 bottom; **courtesy Smith & Hawken:** 3 bottom left, 137, 150 top right and bottom left, 151 top right, 153 bottom left; **Holly Stewart:** 11; **Thomas J. Story:** 39 left, 102 bottom, 116 left; **Friedrich Strauss/The Garden Picture Library:** 145 top center; **Friedrich Strauss/M.A.P.:** 49 top and bottom, 96 top and bottom; **Tim Street-Porter:** cover, 8 bottom, 14 bottom, 23; **Ron Sutherland/ The Garden Picture Library:** 13 bottom, 15 top left, 101 right; **Brigitte Thomas/The Garden Picture Library:** 27 top; **Michael S. Thompson:** 50 right, 87 bottom, 117 right, 146 bottom right, 147 top left; **courtesy unicahome.com:** 151 bottom right; **Jared Vermeil:** 77, 80–81 all; **Deidra Walpole Photography:** 21, 24 left, 26 bottom right, 31, 66 bottom, 75, 79 top left, 103 top, 109 right; **Judy White/GardenPhotos.com:** 12, 50 left, 57–59, 63, 79 bottom left, 83, 88 top center and bottom center, 101 left, 105 bottom, 114, 124 left, 125 right, 129 inset, 135 left and bottom right; **David Winger:** 146 top center; **Karen Witynski Carr:** 1, 22 bottom, 39 right, 100; **Steven Wooster/The Garden Picture Library:** 34 right

acknowledgments *We would like to extend special thanks to Rob Steiner (robsteinergardens.com), Jared Vermeil (vermeildesign.com), Jeffrey Miller (millercomp.com), Lucy Hardiman, and Mark Morro at Big Sur Media (coastalgardener.com). Thanks also to the staff of* Sunset *magazine.*

index